Who's Going To Get Gomer?

Who's Going To Get Gomer?

Janice Fountaine

Printed in the United States of America

Publishing services by Selah Publishing Group, LLC, Tennessee. The views expressed or implied in this work do not necessarily reflect those of Selah Publishing Group.

ISBN 978-1-58930-186-3
Library of Congress Control Number: 2007901345

This book is dedicated to the Body of Christ.
May we all come to know Him and
the power of His resurrection.

This book is dedicated to the Gomers of this world,
the broken and the lost.
The church is going to get you.

Acknowledgements

I acknowledge God the Father, God the Son and God the Holy Spirit as the one and only sovereign God. The alpha and the Omega, the beginning and the end. The I Am that I Am. Awesome, all powerful, all knowing, besides Him, there is no other.

I thank my husband, Darnell Fountaine, my mother Lenora Battle, and the members and partners of Kingdom Empowerment Church and Ministries for their encouragement and support.

Contents

Introduction

It was a cold wintry night in an inner city of the United States. A young woman sat in what was once the multipurpose room of an elementary school. Her light brown hair was swung back off of her head and gathered together in the back by a ponytail holder.

She sat slumped down in a child-sized metal chair and listened attentively to the speaker, who was in the process of giving a synopsis of her life story. As the speaker came to a close and stepped down from the podium, the young woman sat up in her chair and raised her hand. She had been anticipating this very moment. The moderator beckoned her to come forward, and she did.

She rose from her chair and began to move to the front of the room. Her dry, lifeless skin looked as if it had once been healthy and beautiful, but lack of care seemed to have taken its toll. Her slender, underweight body appeared to be moving too slow for her mind, as preconceived thoughts of what she was about to say raced through her head. However, the young woman had determined to make it to the front of the room, no matter how reluctant her weakened body was.

She stepped up to the podium and looked out over the audience and into their faces, and then she began to speak:

"Hello, my name is Gomer, and I am a prostitute. I have been unfaithful to my husband, and I have left him, along with our three children. And now I want to go back home. I know I have messed up, but I still want to go back home. I have offended the very one who has cared for and protected me. I have put myself and others before him. I have grieved him so much, but I am sorry and I am tired and I do not want to be here anymore.

"So, as I was sitting back there, which is what I have been doing for quite awhile now, I decided to come forward and ask you for a favor.

"I cannot get out of this situation by myself. I just do not have the strength. So, I was wondering if, when you leave here and go to your various destinations, you would ask around for me. Ask someone. Ask anyone. Who's going to get Gomer? Who is going down to the shelters, the crack houses, the transition homes, the abandoned school buildings, the prisons, and even the churches to rescue the broken and the lost? Tell them that I really do not want to be in this condition or situation any longer, but I need help. I am lost, and I need a lot of help getting out of my situation.

"Yes, tell them that Gomer said that she is too weak to come out on her own. She just does not have the courage or the strength to do it alone. She needs someone, anyone, someone stronger than herself and her problem to come and get her.

"Tell them that it has been year after year, and still no one has come for her. Tell them that Gomer said she is easy to recognize. She is the one who has been beaten, misused, and abused. She is the one with the chains about her wrists and feet. She is the one who has been bound and confused, as if left for dead. She is the one with the tear-stained face. She is the one with the low self-esteem. She is the one who may appear to look okay, but in reality, she is broken, she is lost, and she does not want to be in this situation anymore."

The young woman paused and, with her head held down, ended by saying, "Well, that is all that I have to say. Remember, ask them, ask anyone, Who's going to get Gomer?"

Body of Christ, this woman represents so many people. She represents so many broken and lost people throughout this world whom God has commissioned you and me, the Church, the Body of Christ, the *ecclesia*, to go out and get. Yes, we are to go and find the Gomers of this world, the broken and the lost. The prostitutes, the imprisoned, the drug addicts, the alcoholics, the abused, our friends, our coworkers and family members—we have been mandated to go and set them free from the bondages of sin. The bondages of bad decisions and low self-esteem. The bondages of mental, physical, and emotional abuse; molestation; rejection; sexual perversion; unforgiveness; deceit; pride; and self-depravation. Those of us who believe that Jesus Christ is the only begotten Son of God and that God raised Him from the dead have been mandated to rescue them from the clutches of sin by bringing them into a saving relationship with God and empowering them to fulfill God's purpose in their lives.

This woman, Gomer, asks the question for which so many are crying unto God to give them an answer: "Who's going to get me out of this bondage?"

My brothers and sisters in Christ Jesus, I heard the Spirit of God asking the Church, "Who is going to get Gomer? Who dares to come out of their religious comfort zones, become empowered, and breathe life into these dry places?"

God has created and commanded us to go and get the broken and the lost. He has given us the authority to bind and to loose, to exercise power over all the works of the enemy. Yet the broken are still broken, and the Church, the Body of Christ, is underachieving and under-producing.

The Church is very visible in the pulpits. They are very visible sitting on the deacons' row, the ushers' bench, and in the choir's loft. They are very visible sporting their bishops' rings, choir robes, ushers' pins, and trustees' hats. Yet Gomer cannot see them. They are not as visible where Gomer is. As a result, Gomer sits waiting and wondering, even crying out, "Who's going to rescue me?"

Body of Christ, God is not pleased with the Church's performance, and we must do something about it.

I have written this book because God has given me a mandate to sound an alarm to you—an alarm with which I am sure many who operate in the gift of the prophet are finding themselves impregnated, as well. This book has been written out of obedience to the voice and unction of the Spirit of God to write and speak forth what the Lord our God is saying to the Church.

This alarm, which must be sound, will:

- Help bring many Christians into a more intimate relationship with God.
- Help Christians understand what God expects from them in relation to the broken people of this world.
- Help Christians understand that God is not pleased with the condition of the Church.
- Help Christians understand that God is not pleased with the condition of the broken and that the Church is being held accountable for them.

- Help Christians see where they are in relation to where they should be in accessing and operating in Kingdom authority.
- Help Christians understand that they are moving at a disappointing pace in harvesting the broken and the lost.
- Help Christians understand that God is not only displeased with the rate in which they are harvesting the lost, but the quality in which they are nourishing them, as well.

This book will show the Body of Christ that they must:

1. Hear the voice of God and obey.
2. Walk in an intimate relationship with Him.
3. Understand the concept of divine purpose.
4. Understand the principle of walking in Kingdom authority.
5. Speak life into the lives of the broken and the lost.

My People, No Glory

And he said, "Please, show me Your glory."
Exodus 33:18

The book of Hosea, written by the prophet Hosea, the son of Beeri, rings with the great aura of God the Father's love for a people, Israel. A people who had wandered away from Him. A people who, despite God's numerous attempts to display His love for them, rejected Him. A people who, despite the manifestation of God's mighty power, went away satisfied with mere works without seeking to drink from the water brooks of His glory.

God's chosen people, Israel, never consistently longed for His presence. They never consistently longed for His manifested glory in them. So, as a people, they never really experienced His glory, the very essence of Him, the way God wanted them to. As a people, despite all that was before them and all that was available to them, they did not seek His glory either individually or corporately. As a result, they could not be faithful to Him.

Their most humble leader, Moses, was able to see the glory of God because he asked for it and longed for it. He realized that, outside the mighty acts of God, was laid the opportunity to fellowship with Him and come into an intimate relationship that far exceeded the experience and benefits of those mighty acts.

Moses witnessed the plagues, and he saw the parting of the Red Sea, just as Israel did. Yet in Exodus 33:18, he is recorded as having asked to see the glory of God. He realized that the *glory* of God was different from the *acts* of God.

Many will witness the mighty acts, but not all will come to intimately know the God of the mighty acts. Oh yes, many have experienced full-grown cancers healed, limbs restored, the dead come to life, but still they do not yearn to see God's glory. They do not long to know Him, the power behind the acts and the works.

Many will argue that the mighty acts of God are His glory. But, in essence, they are the manifestation of His glory. I heard Benny Hinn state "His glory is Himself," and I agree. It is His person, His presence upon and within us. The manifestation of God's anointing and the experience of His power upon a situation or an event is a by-product of the glory of God. It is a by-product of Him. It is a by-product of who He is. It is a by-product of the very essence of Him. It is a by-product of His anointing and His attributes, His thoughts, His ways, His acts that have saturated and permeated our bodies, souls, and spirits. Therefore, the ones who possess the qualities and attributes of God are those who have seen His glory. And to know Him is to witness the manifestation of Him and all that is Him.

To know the very person of God Himself makes us, despite our human frailties and errors, seek to be in His presence and to know His thoughts and His ways. Yes, we will seek to think His thoughts and to move and act in situations the same way that He does. To do this, we must realize that there is so much more to God than signs and wonders.

We must know that there is a place of intimacy in Him that can hardly be explained, yet we cannot live without it. It becomes as necessary and habitual as eating and sleeping. It is as natural and as second nature to us as inhaling and exhaling. It is a lifestyle that, if missed or neglected, would cause us to become spiritually dysfunctional and dormant.

Seeing God's glory causes us to experience an intimacy, a closeness to Him, that in turn makes us realize that we will never be alone and that we can never do without it. It produces an assurance, a protection, an awareness, a confidence, and a surety, a knowing that goes far beyond anything that we will ever experience outside of God.

It assures us of our love and devotion to God, as well as God's love and faithfulness to us. Israel's neglect in seeking to experience the glory of God caused them to wander and thus become unfaithful to Him.

The State of Gomer

> All we like sheep have gone astray; we have turned, every one, to his own way; and the LORD has laid on Him the iniquity of us all.
>
> Isaiah 53:6

Hosea heeded the command of the Father and did what he was told. He illustrated the relationship between Israel and God by choosing to marry a prostitute named Gomer, which, by interpretation, means "ruin and corruption." She was the daughter of Diblaim, which, by interpretation, means "two cakes or lumps of figs." Israel was as sheep gone astray. They had gone from a condition of plenty, green pastures, abundance, and more than enough to a condition of ruin and corruption. They had gone from worshiping a loving, providing God to worshiping an unloving, unproviding idol.

Hosea's experience with Gomer was meant to illustrate the grief that God felt, as anyone would feel, when He found Himself being cheated on by someone whom He loved immensely. He was grieved by having to watch Israel, whom He loved and who was known to be His people, reject Him.

Israel—unfaithful, idol-worshiping Israel—needed to see their offenses against God and that, in their offenses came their self-inflicted ruin.

By society's standards, Gomer was a nobody. She was of low social and economic status. She was a loser, so to speak. By many people's account, she represented a person who never had achieved anything in life—and never would. She depicted someone who had reached a point of no return, a point of "it's too late." It appeared that she would never amount to anything, or, even if she did straighten up, it would be too late to make anything of herself.

In much the same way that Gomer represented the state and condition of Israel, she also depicts the state, condition, and plight of the broken and the lost today. Nothing much has changed; mankind is prone to wander, and wander we have.

Within the walls of sanctuaries throughout the world, at any given time, many Christians are either sitting next to a previous Gomer, or within their homes, they are living with one. They are definitely sharing the same buses, boardrooms, or lunch counters with a Gomer. Whatever the case, there are Gomers in our midst. They are all around us, and we, the Body of Christ, have a responsibility to them and an accountability to God; therefore, we must do something about it.

Everyone has been given the opportunity for salvation: "If you confess with your mouth the Lord Jesus and believe in your heart that God has raised Him from the dead, you will be saved" (Romans 10:9). We have all been given access to eternal and everlasting life free from the presence of sin and in the presence of God. We grieve the One, God the Father, who has offered it to us through Jesus Christ. We grieve the One who loves us beyond reason and understanding. We deny His existence and long for another. We allow ourselves to become slaves to sin and act as though we enjoy every moment of it. We do not realize, until we are beyond escape, that we have been duped. We do not admit it, until sin has made a prostitute out of us, that perhaps we have made a mistake. We say, "Maybe things have gotten out of control," or, "Maybe I have bitten off more than I can chew." But in reality, we do not realize the pit that we have allowed the enemy to throw us in, until sin has sapped us of any energy that we may have had to raise ourselves up and out of it. In this pit, the lack of light makes us spiritually immune to the dangers that lie within its depths. We become conditionally unable to differentiate between light and darkness. Because of this inability, we are not able to make a conscious decision about our lives or the direction in which we should go. We become totally dependent on people and substances to hide our shame and sorrow. We become totally dependent on drugs and alcohol or unhealthy and unproductive relationships, and the result is low self-esteem, emotional and physical abuse, neglect, and rejection. We are unable to hide our shame and pull ourselves out of the pit. We allow ourselves to be placed in bondage by the very things that the enemy prides himself on using to oppress, depress, suppress, and possess us.

Gomer represents a condition that every one of us has been in at some point in our lives. We were enslaved to sin. But for those of us who are born again, there was a Hosea. He showed up at a very pivotal and crucial point in our lives to rescue us and bring us into relationship with our Lord and Savior, Jesus Christ.

Someone heard God speak and went out and got us. Despite the uncompassionate advice and cries from others, someone went out to the street corner, rehab center, crack house, or prison under the yoke-breaking power and anointing of God and brought us back. They brought us to God with long, sacrificial hours of witnessing, laboring, fervent worship and prayers, and an empowered, anointed life that was surrendered to the will of God.

It is true: Jesus Christ paid the price for us to be brought back into fellowship with God. But we must turn away from sin to gain this access. We must exercise our free will, and for those who do not know this, someone must tell them. Telling them includes going into the enemy's camp and making this known to the broken and the lost. It includes setting them free from enslavement so that they can hear and receive this great salvation, which is available to them through the birth, life, death, burial, resurrection, and ascension of Jesus Christ, the only begotten Son of God.

So many do not know that they can truly be set free from the bondage of sin. And when they do learn this, they do not have the strength on their own to raise themselves up and out of the depths of its clutches. The natural realm is no match against the supernatural realm. This is why, when believers try to disciple the lost, we must go empowered, or our going is superficial and of no real effect at all.

The broken and the lost, those who are out of fellowship and unsaved, do not understand how much they need God reigning in their lives. Most have no concept whatsoever about the serious and astonishing reality of the supernatural. And if the truth be told, many saved people do not, either. Many Christians' belief in the supernatural does not go past their belief in God. And even then, it is to a limited degree and in a limited realm. This realm is often experienced only as far as their natural reasoning will allow them to comprehend it. This is because they have not been in fellowship with God on a consistent, high-quality basis to believe otherwise.

The Gomers lay in their unfaithful, adulterous, idol-worshiping posture while God is speaking to the Church to go and take them by force from the enemy. But we are corporately unresponsive. We do not realize that God will go to any means necessary again and again to reach the lost, the backslidden, the unsaved, the wandering, the abused, the abusing, the confused, the misused, the weak, the poor, the untrained, and the untamed. God's love reaches down into the pits, the cracks, and the crevices of the kingdoms of the world and reclaims souls from the monstrous, unloving, slave master named

Sin. Sin is the devil's tool for mankind's destruction. Sin's chains are unclenching and cannot be penetrated in the natural. Its noose about the neck cannot be untied.

Where Sin goes, you go. Where it lies, you lie. What it feeds on, you feed on. Without Jesus Christ, you belong to Sin, and the only one who does not realize it is you.

Who Is Able to Go?

> Jesus said, "Go therefore and make disciples of all the nations, baptizing them in the name of the Father and of the Son and of the Holy Spirit."
>
> Matthew 28:19

The only power greater than sin and Satan is the power of God. It is the only thing that can release the lost and broken from the clutches of sin, demonic oppression, and possession. This power is the yoke-breaking anointing that is available to every Christian to free the broken and the lost from the chains of the devil and enable them to fulfill God's purpose for their lives.

This power is accessed in the Kingdom realm of God. When we access this power, we take on the authority and rulership of the kingdom of earth and the world. We are empowered to walk in Kingdom authority. With this empowerment come all the tools necessary to do what we must do to dominate earth and all of the demonic powers illegally invading it.

Only those who have been anointed and empowered by the Holy Spirit can rescue, restore, and reconcile the broken and the lost to their estranged love, God.

Church of God, Body of Christ, those who are called to bring about this reconciliation are you and me. God has made Himself clear, and we must obey. We must go and get Gomer. We are an extension of Jesus Christ. Apostles, prophets, evangelists, pastors, and teachers have been given the extension gifts because we are an extension of Jesus Christ. We are to prophetically teach, train, transfer, and impart ministry gifts to the Body. In John 14:12, Jesus clearly proclaimed, "Most assuredly, I say to you, He who believes in Me, the works that I do he will do also; and greater works than these he will do, because I go to My Father." This transfer took place so that we would be equipped to seek and save the lost and glorify the Father while doing it. Jesus glorified the Father by making salvation possible. He put man in right relationship with the Father. We have been gifted by Jesus and the Holy Spirit to seek the lost, compel the lost (which encompasses spiritual warfare), save the lost, and make disciples (which includes empowerment and impartation). We must go and get His adulterous lover. We must go and get the backslidden, the broken, and the lost. We must go and get the ones whom He shed His blood for, so that they could be reconciled to the Father.

Body of Christ, go to the drug and alcohol demons and command them to let God's people go. Speak to those powers and principalities, and set the lost free. Set them free from the chains of low self-esteem; fornication; adultery; rejection; physical, emotional, and mental abuse; deceit; self-depravation; stealing; strife; and murder.

Body of Christ, unlock the doors of demonic infiltration and possession and take Gomer back. But do not be astonished when you have to take her by force. You must be prepared to do so. This is why we have access to so great a power and authority. We have Kingdom anointing and authority. Spiritual warfare dictates that we operate in supernatural power. So, go to the marketplace, go wherever Gomer is, and take her back.

If she is in the crack house, go!
If she is on the street corner, go!
If she is in the mental institution, go!

If she is in the prison, go!
If she is in the rehab center, go!
If she is at your job, go!
If she is in your home, go!
If she is in the Church, go!

Wherever she is, Body of Christ, we must go. And we must go now.

We must go with the power, the yoke-breaking anointing of God. We must be empowered, or we will not get her back. There will only be the appearance of deliverance. The enemy will not take us seriously. The enemy must recognize Kingdom authority in us or our works will be of ill effect to the Kingdom and to Gomer's life.

Jesus purchased her with His life; now we must take her back with His Spirit.

We must apply the blood of Jesus Christ and speak in His name. At the name of Jesus Christ, every knee shall bow, and every tongue, both natural and supernatural, must confess that Jesus Christ is Lord. (see Philippians 2:10)

Remember also, you cannot use what you do not have. You cannot use the power of God to get Gomer if you have not gone into the Kingdom realm and accessed this power. You cannot compromise God's Word by sleeping with the enemy and living an unrighteous life. That is a wile of the devil. The blood of Jesus Christ can only be used by those who walk in holiness before God. That is a prerequisite. It is possible to misrepresent the blood of Jesus Christ, but you cannot misuse it and think that it is going to release power for you. It must be applied through holy living, or it will not work for you. You cannot mix the natural with the supernatural and think that Gomer is going to be set free.

God does not need the world's strategies to get Gomer. He must use His vessels. He must use His Church, His anointed Body. We must be empowered, and we must speak to the mountains in the lives of the broken and the lost. Church of God, we cannot deal with powers and principalities, spiritual wickedness in high places, without the enabling grace and power of the Holy Spirit.

You must tap into the supernatural dimension and realm that God established in you while you were in your mother's womb. You must find out where you are to go and walk in Kingdom authority. There is no time to waste. Gomer is dying, but she wants to live. She has to live. God has ordained her from her mother's womb to live. He has declared that Gomer shall live!

The State of the Church Today

> For whom He foreknew, He also predestined to be conformed to the image of His Son, that He might be the first among many brethren.
>
> Romans 8:29

The relationship between the Christian Church and their God is a love affair gone sour. As a matter of fact, this relationship has gone underdeveloped for some and completely undeveloped for others. The Church has fooled itself into thinking that it can be in fellowship with the world's system and its god and give God the leftovers. Then they try to move and operate in His power and authority and dominate the earth with a "leftover mentality." They believe that they can give God leftover time at the end of the day, the month, and the year. They try to give Him their leftover talents after they have prostituted this talent to the devil, and they offer their leftover treasure after they have fulfilled the lust of their own eyes. And then they proclaim that they have a relationship with God. They testify on Sunday mornings that they are saved, sanctified, filled with the Holy Ghost, and fire-baptized. How can this be, when God has gotten nothing but leftovers? How can this be, when God wants and requires first fruits?

Our appetites for the ungodly things of life, such as music and television, are a stench to His nostrils. The Church has gone about acting as if everything is all right. They are acting as if everything is peachy keen, if you please, between them and God. But in reality, there is no relationship at all.

We dress like the world, wear our hair like the world, and even expose our bodies like the world. We expose our spirits to whatever the enemy puts before our eyes and our ears. The only ones who are not fooled by our masquerade are God and the world. Yes, the Church has taken on the appearance of the world. Then we try to convince the world that we are holy and acceptable to God, when in reality, the world, Satan's alliance, does not accept or respect us. The Church mixes with the world, and then acts as if God is supposed to be grateful and accept us as we are.

With the Church, it's too much flesh. Too much attention is given to ourselves and not enough is given to God. And the world is laughing all the way to the bank while we continuously make music and other folly with them.

Wake up, Body, and shake yourself. God is not fooled nor entertained. The relationship between the Church and God has been a tragedy without triumph. We cannot please God, the enemy, and ourselves at the same time. God won't have it.

The Church must step up to the plate. The average Christian appears to be out of fellowship with God and out of touch with the power and the process of brokenness. They are in their own world. It seems as though the life of a Christian has become more of a fad or a tradition, rather than a Spirit-led lifestyle.

The world, it seems, has lost respect for the Church. They cannot tell the difference between it and themselves. Many people argue that they do not want the Church's God. Why should they? They say that He cannot keep His own body holy.

The Body of Christ is out of order. We are not in coordination with our Head. We have neglected our own souls and are not walking in the spiritual authority that Jesus Christ has made available to us. This authority gives the Body access to the same power to which God gave Jesus access. The gospel according to John 14:12 records Jesus passing this power on to the Church, so that we could walk victoriously in our own lives and empower the lost to do the same.

The Church is walking in disobedience because we have refused to obey God by going to get the broken and the lost. We have neglected to go and get Gomer out of the crack houses, prisons, foster homes, shelters, rehab centers, and even our own bedrooms and boardrooms. Romans 8:29 lets us know that we have been predestined to be conformed to the image of our Lord and Savior, Jesus Christ. Our conformity is not just so that we would experience salvation, but so that we would be instrumental in helping others experience its power, as well.

There is a sad, striking correlation between the number of churches open as opposed to the number of souls lost and broken in America today. The attitude of the lost toward the Church is so negative that we have to break certain demonic and relational barriers before we can even give them the salvation plan. We want to feed them Romans 10:9–10, but in reality, they are not able to digest the plan of salvation. The Church must first straighten out the negative publicity, which we have brought on ourselves and God as a result of our unholy and unrighteous living and behavior before the lost.

Quite frankly, many of the broken are backsliders. They are victims of church strife, harassment, embarrassment, neglect, misunderstandings, and a lack of spiritual nourishment and empowerment.

Apostles, prophets, evangelists, pastors, and teachers, hear the word of the Lord: God is not pleased with us. We are not rearing saints. We are not rearing Kingdom builders. We are rearing and nourishing carnal Christians. We pacify, not purify, them, and they have become clueless about what God really wants, expects, and commands of them. They have become people-driven as opposed to purpose-driven.

Many people are going to their graves without fulfilling God's purpose for their lives because we have preferred that they stay as laity instead of raising an Aaron's army.

We never trained and nurtured them into becoming the warriors that the Kingdom of God dictated that they be. They never tapped into the yoke-breaking anointing that they needed to walk in to experience supernatural prosperity and peace. They never sowed into the vineyard, as laborers sent by the Lord of the harvest. Many never realized the peace, power, prosperity, potential, or perspective of being in an intimate relationship with the only true and living God.

Body of Christ, God is sounding an alarm throughout the walls of our churches and commanding us to lay aside the business of the world and go and get Gomer. Yes, we are too busy. We are too busy with the comings and goings of church and home life, that we forget about Kingdom building and give little thought to the Gomers of this world. If the truth be told, too many Christians are living with Gomer-like symptoms themselves. There are too many Christians who are walking in low self-esteem, lack of provision, unforgiveness, adultery, fornication, biblical error, unrighteousness, and the like. Many look and act like Gomer, yet they are confessing to be saved and sanctified. Some so-called seasoned Christians are even still being taught the principles of salvation when, in reality, they should have long been off the milk of the Gospel and moving in the realms of Kingdom authority. They should be on the meat of the Gospel by now. They should have long matured to the higher dimensions of Christianity, which is where they become empowered to minister to the broken and the lost.

How is it, one might ask, and the Church certainly should be asking this question, that there are so many lost souls in our world, while so many church doors remain open? How is it that there is such an alarming number of broken people in and out of the Church, yet the Church, the Body of Christ, walks about calm and clueless? They move about while comfortable and satisfied, acting as if the only thing left to be done here on earth is for Jesus Christ to return and rapture the Church.

Isn't the Church God's mouthpiece?
Isn't the Church God's vessel?
Isn't the Church a reflection of God's image?
Isn't the church God's tool in the world?
Isn't the Church God's source to reap the harvest?
Isn't the church the epitome of God Himself?
Isn't the Church the power vein of the manifestation of God's mighty acts?

How can it be that the Church is in such a comfortable state, when so many are broken and lost in the world?

How is it that we have convinced ourselves to believe that God feels good about our productivity rate in regard to Kingdom building?

How do we think that God feels about our performance? We certainly cannot think that God is satisfied with us. We cannot think that God is satisfied with our so-called spirituality. We cannot think that God is satisfied with our ways of doing things.

Certainly, we cannot believe that God is satisfied with us as a Body, as His vessels. We cannot be fooled into thinking that God is pleased with us. We cannot have convinced ourselves to believe that God is pleased with our performance. No, men and women of God, we cannot.

The truth of the matter is that over two thousand years ago, God spoke to the Church and commanded it to "go therefore and make disciples of all the nations, baptizing them in the name of the Father and of the Son and of the Holy Ghost" (Matthew 28:19). Yet, here we are today, moving about as if we have not heard Him at all.

We use worldly entertainment, for example, to lure the lost. We act as if God is not smart or powerful enough to draw them to Himself without our compromising antics. We have convinced the world and ourselves that the only way that God can win the lost is through compromise.

My brothers and sisters in Christ Jesus, hear the word of the Lord. The Church is walking a thin line with God. The Church has hidden the truth about God in unrighteousness, while the lost are walking about in darkness, yearning to see the light.

What is wrong? Where has the Church erred? What is it that has prevented the Church from fulfilling God's Kingdom purpose in the world today?

The Power of Fellowship

> Jesus said, "My sheep hear my voice, and I know them, and they follow Me."
>
> John 10:27

When he heard God speak, Hosea was able to do what he did because he was in relationship with God. He knew God's voice, and because he did, Hosea had no problem obeying God.

I contend that the fundamental and underlying problem with the Church's lack of fulfillment of God's purpose in the world is the absence of an authentic relationship with God. This lack of relationship has contributed to the overall inability to operate in the dimensions and realms of Kingdom authority. As a result, the Church, both corporately and individually, has been hindered from determining God's will, as well as measuring the depths of His expectations concerning the fulfillment of His purpose in them. They have made the same mistake that Paul pointed out to the early Church in Romans 1–3. They have overestimated the depth of their spirituality and underestimated the height of God's expectations of them.

This inability to operate has been initiated by God's refusal to empower a Body that is not in relationship with Him. An absence of relationship with God has produced a catastrophic barrier, which has lined the hearts and souls of many believers throughout the Body of Christ. It has prevented the Church from hearing God, from accessing Kingdom resources and power, and from discovering and fulfilling God's purpose.

The fundamental component that would put us into relationship with the Father, so that we can walk in agreement with Him, is fellowship. Fellowship with the Holy Spirit breeds an intimate relationship with God and allows us to hear God and walk in Kingdom authority.

Fellowship goes beyond friendship and fascination. You see, God is not trying to be your "buddy," or to entertain you, or to keep you happy as the world knows happiness. God seeks to conform the Church to His image with the specific intent to win the lost so that we can get out of here and enter into the realm of eternity.

Body of Christ, we must do something about this tragedy. We are out of relationship with the harvest and the Lord of the harvest.

It is fellowship that brings us into relationship with God. It is in this fellowship that we will be able to differentiate between the voice of God, the voice of the enemy, or even our own needy, demanding flesh.

The voice of God is not one that can be easily recognized. Despite what has been declared throughout sanctuaries and conference centers, God's voice is not recognizable without fellowship. Where there is an absence of fellowship, there is a Christian who cannot differentiate between the voice of God and the other voices that they hear. This is why so many Christians err in what they believe they hear from God.

Many of us go through our lives without understanding that the voice we think we hear is not God's voice at all, but instead a voice that reigns in the life of any individual who lacks fellowship with God. We must be in fellowship with God to learn or even come close to mastering the sound of God's still, small, loving, peaceful, yet authoritative, no-nonsense voice. If we cannot differentiate between the voices that we hear within ourselves, we will surely err in our obedience to God and the choices and decisions that we make in life.

The voice of the enemy works in coordination with our fleshly desires. He taps into and comes into agreement with our carnal man. He makes sure that he carefully and discreetly lines the infiltrating thoughts that he suggests to us with the desires and manipulations of our flesh's emotions, lack of wisdom, and lack of knowledge of God's will for us. This lack is fueled by the absence of fellowship with God.

Our inner voice speaks through the desires of the flesh, which is empowered or denied according to our ability and consistency in placing it under authority to the will of God for us as Christians. This absolutely cannot be obtained unless we are in constant and consistent fellowship with the Father.

We hear the Father speak to us in our spirits, which He has given to us so that we can communicate with Him through the Holy Spirit. God is a Spirit and will only communicate with us by and through His Spirit to our spirit man.

The enemy, being a spirit, as well, possesses, suppresses, oppresses, and depresses an individual. This is why we have been biblically instructed to "let this mind be in you that was in Christ Jesus" (see Philippians 2:5). This is why we are biblically instructed to put "every thought that enters our mind under subjection to the will of Jesus Christ" (see 2 Corinthians 10:5). If a thought gets past our minds, then into our spirits it goes. Whatever reaches fruition in the mind is what will nourish the heart and govern the spirit. This will be reflected in our attitudes, speech, mannerisms, and behavior.

We, as beings who have been given free will, acknowledge and obey either the desires of the spirit or of the flesh. The one or the other is what we will be in communication and relationship with. It is because of these two that we become moved and motivated by the voices that we hear.

Oh yes, I can hear God speak. But I can hear the enemy speak and my own inner voice speak, as well. The voices we hear are not all the same. And if we cannot differentiate between the voices that we hear, we will surely err and sin.

This is why God promotes fellowship and relationship between Himself and His Body. Fellowship is the coming together of two or more individuals on an ongoing, consistent, constant, repetitive basis for a specific purpose relative to the developing, maintaining, promoting, and demonstration of the relationship.

It is out of this relationship that God will communicate with us. He will reveal His will to us and manifest His power through us. He will make plain His mighty works and show us His glory, which is Himself. He will make known, clear, direct, and concise His purpose in us to win the lost and promote His Kingdom.

God rejects anything other than fellowship with Himself because:

1. Without it, we cannot come into relationship with Him, and
2. Without relationship, we will not be able to discern the voice of the Holy Spirit from the other voices that we hear.

If a person cannot hear God and recognize His voice, then he cannot be in agreement with Him. He cannot know His will or obey Him.

But if he is in relationship with God, then when he hears Him speak, he will:

1. Recognize His voice.
2. Listen to Him.
3. Be attentive.
4. Obey him.

At this point, he will not be concerned with or wait to determine who, what, when, where, how, and why. He will simply know that he heard God speak, and he will obey.

Once you have learned to reject, cast down, and put under submission thoughts that are not of God but of the enemy, half the battle is over. The other half is within yourself.

Once you have died to yourself and put your flesh under subjection, then the other half of the battle is won. You must die to yourself. Your untimely, unreasonable, and unprofitable desires, as well as your childish ways of saying and doing things, must be put to death and placed under the subjection of the Word and will of God.

You must understand and be aware that the enemy, as well as your flesh wants you to follow them. They will have you on an emotional roller coaster if you put them in charge. It will seem as though they are out of control and will not stop. Up and down; up and down. No stability. No clear direction.

But when you are in fellowship with God, you cannot be tricked by the enemy or by your flesh. Instead, you are in agreement with your Creator. And when God speaks, what He says goes unchallenged, whether you fully understand it or not. Your understanding is not predicated on your ability to comprehend in the natural, but to believe and obey in the supernatural.

We do not fully understand God's fervor concerning the lost, but when Hosea heard God speak, God said, "Go and get her again." Yes, Hosea may have thought that it sounded ridiculous, even like a waste of time and effort. Go and get Gomer again? Despite all that she had done to him and against him, he was to go and get her.

I can imagine God saying to Hosea, and to you and me, "I still love her. I know that you may not understand how I could still love and desire an adulterous wife, but I do. She is tied to Me. How is that? you might ask. You see, there is still some of Me inside of her. No matter how she looks, how she acts, who she's worshiping. I created her, and I predestined her to be conformed to the image of Jesus Christ. I created her in My image. Go and get her. When I see her, I see Myself. There is still some of Me inside of her because I formed her in My image. I knew her before she was in her mother's womb. (see Jeremiah 1:5) I made her. I deposited My Spirit in her. I am in covenant relationship with the Me inside of her. You don't see Me in her, but My love is there, My patience is there, My long-suffering is there, My revelation knowledge is predestined to be there.

"Yes, go and get Gomer, Hosea, Body of Christ, you whom I have called. You who recognize My voice and when you hear Me speak, dare to obey Me.

"Go and get Gomer, the prostitute, the broken. The abused and the misused. The molested and the neglected. The seemingly unprotected. Those with the poor self-image and low self-esteem. The drug addicts, the alcoholics, the proud, the hopeless, the homeless, the sick and depraved, the weak, the insecure, the afflicted, the rejected, the lost, the unsaved, the backsliders. Go and get her. Go and get her now.

"I can hear their mothers crying,
Their grandmothers praying,
Their children screaming,
Their moaning and groaning.
'Who's coming for me?' they are crying.
Who's going to get Gomer?"

The instructive voice of God is often heard during times when we least expect to hear from Him. He may come while we are engaged in almost any task. He comes speaking in a still, small, but authoritative tone when there are instructions to be heard. He intrudes on our thoughts and petitions and makes His will known to us. We can discern His comfort and assurance while at the same time reverently knowing and respecting the fact that we are being given an uncompromising command by One who does not acknowledge the words "no," "maybe," "let me think about it," or anything of the like. In this realm, we enter into intimacy with God in which we long for and reverence His presence and His closeness, while at the same time knowing that His presence has come for a specific reason and that God's will must not and cannot be taken lightly.

This is a point in your relationship at which it becomes clear that God is the Creator and you are the creature. You long for His daily presence, and you are no longer surprised when you find yourself in it, almost at the very thought of Him. You are consumed by His love and purpose in you, and you move throughout each day with your thoughts habitually yielded to His Word, His will, and His principles and precepts. You are aware of how He thinks, and your thoughts have become His thoughts because you have mastered rejecting and putting under subjection to Him any thoughts that are not from Him. You think like Him. You walk and move like Him throughout the day. You know that at any given time, you may be prompted by His manifested presence in and around you.

You are aware of spiritual attacks because of where you are in Him. Demons do not like to be around you because of the abiding presence of God. The presence of God causes demons to tremble and flee. They are uncomfortable. They are aware that they cannot share the same atmosphere with holiness. They know that they cannot occupy a space where the presence of God abides. It is understood that they must leave. So they tend to shy away from you. The demons who dare to challenge you or come close to you are those who are working on weapons to deter or frustrate you. They are warfare demons or principalities who are there to do warfare with you in the realm to which you have been elevated. They are not counting on your knowing and being confident that "greater is He that is in you than he that is in the world" (see 1 John 4:4). They are not counting on your being confident that "no weapon that is formed against you will prosper" (see Isaiah 54:17). Instead, they bank on your becoming distracted by their weapons and thus losing the intensity of God's presence. They count on you to doubt and disbelieve where you are in God and not utilize the mantle in which you have been given the anointing and authority and resources to operate.

But when you are in a certain dimension or realm in God, your life, motives, and movements are motivated by what you hear from Him.

Fellowship brings us into the knowledge of God's purpose in us. Once a person realizes and understands the concept of divine purpose, God will reveal, to an individual, his assignment and certain tasks associated with it.

We all must understand that God knew us before we were in our mothers' wombs. Because of His omniscience, God embedded within us certain spiritual gifts, as well as natural talents and knacks for doing things, specifically designed to enhance and support the purpose that He has placed inside of us. While in our mother's womb, God anointed us and set a season for His presence relative to His purpose and relationship with us.

When you have been made aware of your divine purpose and God has revealed your major assignment, He must manifest His presence to you. There is a need for constant communication with you because you could not receive the total vision at one time; you could not handle it. Your flesh would not allow it. Your mortal body limits you to some degree.

With your assignment, there are, attached to it, commissions that vary upon completion and seasons of the Kingdom of God. God has set seasons that are attached to Kingdom building, and if you are not moving at the right pace, He will help you along so that the Kingdom will advance. God's purpose in you is tied to Kingdom building, so God will allow a storm to rise. Yes, He will. He will cause a boisterous wind to disturb the waves on a calm sea. He'll create a fish to accommodate you. He'll make you sour and tasteless to this same hungry fish, causing its belly to ache to the point of regurgitation.

When you come out, no matter how painful and stinking the experience was, you'll admit it was time well spent, and you will acknowledge and proclaim that there is a realm in God where yes, no, or compromise are no longer options. When God speaks, you will simply obey. God will give you a preview of hell, and you will realize that anywhere God sends you and whatever He tells you to do cannot compare to where you just left. You'll come out with a deeper respect for God, and you'll realize the height and depth of His will for His purpose in you to be completed.

Once you realize the concept of divine purpose, then you will understand who you are and why you are the way you are, despite the ups and downs, the ins and outs, and the trials and tribulations of life.

God ordained you and conformed you to His image. He attached you from your mother's womb to His assignment in you. You'll fully understand why you sing like you do, or write, or talk, or administrate, or possess other gifts and personality traits. You will come to the point that you will say, "Now I know who I am and, for the most part, why I act the way I do."

There are some parts of each of us that sin cannot change or destroy. It may distort or camouflage them, but it cannot destroy what God has forbidden to die. Once you realize the concept of divine purpose, you'll also understand that you have been established and set aside for that and that only.

From your mother's womb, grace was given your predestined boundaries and commanded to accommodate you within the scope of your purpose and the realm associated with it.

If your mandate is to pastor a church in a certain area, then grace must see to it that you are able to do and to receive all that is necessary for God's purpose in you to be fulfilled.

Zoning must license you to build. The local advisory neighborhood council must be able to look at you as an asset to the community and not a liability. The local drug addicts must come to you for help and prayer, not having the slightest idea as to why.

Demon forces will continually form weapons against you, only to see them fail. Although it's not here today, provision must come tomorrow, next week, next month, or even next year, but it must come. God's purpose has been established, and these things must come to pass because they are tied to the Kingdom.

If your assignment is to teach on financial prosperity, then grace must deny poverty access to your life once you enter into the realm of financial prosperity. No matter how hard the enemy tries to trick you or break you, grace, or the ability to fulfill God's purpose in you, must deny lack of provision, lack of understanding, and lack of wisdom concerning money matters from infiltrating your assignment.

Why? Not because of you, or any good that you may have done or may be doing. No, not because of your mother or father, but because of your heavenly Father's purpose in you. This purpose is tied to Kingdom building.

Many Christians have not grasped the revelation of Jeremiah 1:5. They have not been taught or made aware of it, or they denied themselves the opportunity to grasp the concept of divine purpose and assignment, power, and grace.

They have not tasted the desire or fulfillment of fulfilling God's purpose in them.

Unless you reach a point in your life where you strive to fulfill God's purpose in you, then there are places, and positions in God that you will never enter into, even though you are well within their grasp. There are dimensions and realms in God that you will never reach unless you are striving to fulfill God's divine purpose in you.

Why? Because in these dimensions and realms lie measures of revelation knowledge that can only be obtained by your seeking to fulfill His purpose in your life and proclaiming, "Thy will be done, Thy Kingdom come on earth, as it is in heaven."

Revelation knowledge encompasses mysteries from heaven and is only released to certain people relative to their purpose and assignment. The release invokes God's will on earth as it is invoked in heaven.

There is no reason for God to release revelation knowledge or manifest His presence on thorny ground. Nothing would be produced or grown.

When you reach the point that you know that you have been created for a purpose, then you innately desire to know more about this purpose. In response to this desire, God calls you into His presence, and while there, reveals to you the specifics of your calling or assignment.

At the same time, you become more aware and knowledgeable of the thoughts and ways of God. You thoroughly understand who the servant is and who the Master is.

Instead of loathing the Master's presence, you long for it. You realize the concept of servanthood and the fact that your relationship with God is completely opposite to that of the world's. Instead of hiding from your Master, you search for Him. You chase Him, because you know that when you see Him, when you come into His presence, you will experience love, peace, comfort, security, and an assurance that you know cannot be provided by any other source, including yourself. When it seems as if your Master has gone away or you feel that He is not close, you pant like a deer pants for the water brooks.

You long for your Master like an infant longs for his mother's milk. You are completely attentive to your Master's whereabouts and totally consumed by your Master's desires and will.

You arise early and go to bed late anticipating your Master's arrival. You disallow unholy thoughts and communication, knowing that they could hinder or even block your ability to hear your Master when He calls or speaks. You are always listening for your Master's call. And when your Master speaks, you hear and obey. You move. Wherever you are and whatever you are doing, you always anticipate and long for your Master's presence.

This is where Hosea was. He was consumed by God's purpose in him. He was consumed by the will of God. Worship and fellowship were necessary and part of his lifestyle. He was aware of God's presence and attentive to His whereabouts. He listened for His voice, knowing that it could and would come at any given time.

I can imagine Hosea saying, "When I heard God speak, I obeyed. When I heard God speak, I knew that what He said was tied to His purpose and His Kingdom."

Hosea's purpose was to illustrate the love of God for His rebellious, faithless, adulterous, idol-worshiping people, Israel. His assignment was to, through his life experience with Gomer, depict a love gone astray, a marriage gone sour. He was to show that despite the unfaithfulness of one, the faithful love of the other remained and prevailed.

When hearing God speak, you must not think about the how or why. You must not try to reason or argue that it does not make sense or that it involves a potentially humiliating task. But when God speaks, you must be experiencing the power of fellowship with Him.

Body of Christ, the power of fellowship is reaped when you are in consistent relationship with God. The power of fellowship is to feel His closeness. The power of fellowship is to hear His voice echoing through your spirit. The power of fellowship is to be able to think about Him and experience His presence almost simultaneously. The power of fellowship is to have a need and know that it is met before you even ask. The power of fellowship is to have a question and have it answered before you even ask the question. The power of fellowship is to think the same thoughts as God. The power of fellowship is to experience the mind of the Father in you. The power of fellowship is to understand that your mind is not in Him, but His mind is in you. His will is your will. Your will is whatever His is at any given time. You look like Him, you act like Him, and you think like Him. You are just like Him. Yet you are not Him. That is the only difference. You are not Him, although you are like Him. The power of fellowship is to know that your purpose is tied to Him. As a matter of fact, it is His purpose in you. And, as I previously mentioned, when you come into this intimate relationship with God, He will make His purpose in you clear and give you the instructions you need. There will be revelation knowledge and unctions from the Holy Spirit that will make you confident of your purpose and of the fact or assurance that you have the grace to fulfill it. The power of God will help you to know that you have all that you need. Whether in the physical or the supernatural realm, you know that it will come. The power of fellowship is to realize and understand that you have been conformed to produce: drawn by the Father, conformed to the Son, and producing by the Spirit (see Psalm 8:30). You will know that you have been created to fulfill God's purpose in you. The power of fellowship is to know that God's purpose in you will always bring reconciliation of the lost to Him.

The power of fellowship is to know that when God is speaking, it is not the time to talk. It is the time to be in a disciplined posture to listen. It is important to learn how to be silent before God. The power of fellowship is to know that when God comes to you, it is for a specific reason, and your soul must be silent in His presence. The power of fellowship is to know that you must put under submission all wandering thoughts, other prayers, and petitions, and hear what God is saying to you. The power of fellowship is being in the right place in God.

When I Heard God Speak

Jesus said, "He who has an ear, let him hear what the Spirit says to the churches."

Revelation 2:7

In Hosea 3:1, when God told Hosea to go again and get Gomer, He was not sending Hosea into unchartered territory. Hosea had been there before—just like the Church has had some affiliation with the broken and the lost. "And such were some of us" (see 1 Corinthians 6:11). If the truth be told, Gomer is an integral part of many of our lives.

For Hosea or anyone else, I suppose, to go the first time and marry Gomer was challenging, but to have to go again, considering all that had happened, was even more difficult. The adulterous affairs, the idolatry, the prostitution, the humiliating position, the abandonment—all of this would cause anyone to be reluctant, to say the least. In fact, many may argue that Hosea's decision was simply stupid. But for Hosea, as it should and must be for the Church, it was about his Master's command, will, and purpose in him.

Hosea's assignment was also to denounce sin and to warn Israel that God was pronouncing judgment on them because of their unfaithfulness to Him. Israel had played the harlot. They had become involved in adulterous affairs with the pagan gods.

Sure, what God told Hosea does not make sense to most of us, but God's thoughts and ways are higher than ours. We cannot comprehend them with our natural understanding and reasoning. We can only understand the thoughts and ways of God if we seek and call upon Him. Then He will make them known to us through the Holy Spirit. Then we will take on His image and be like Him, thinking and acting like Him in any given situation or at any given time. Unless we take on God's image, we will never be able to understand the power and abundance of salvation and fellowship with God. We will never be able to understand or grasp the lengths to which our Father's love for us will go to ensure our eternal and everlasting life.

Sure, what God told Hosea to do probably didn't make sense to Hosea; nor does it make sense to many Christians today. I am convinced that it was nothing that Hosea was going to be able to do on his own. If it were, he probably would have already done it. Hosea, as with any prophet or Christian for that matter, moves by the Spirit. In other words, where the Spirit of God does not lead, you should not go.

What God told Hosea to do, as well as what He has commanded the Church to do, may not seem to bring about benefits or rewards. Hosea's task certainly was not anything to brag about to his friends, nor something that would make his parents or siblings proud. It was not something church folk would consider a good move on his part. It was definitely not a prosperous move. No, it was not to Hosea's advantage at all.

So, what was the motivating factor behind his actions? What was the motivating factor behind going again and getting Gomer? What was the motivating factor behind this courageous, yet embarrassing act of Hosea's, to go again a second time and get someone who had literally broken his heart and then rubbed it in his face?

What is the motivating factor for a person to go again and get someone against all odds, against his better judgment, against the advice of family and friends? What makes someone reject the natural rules of compassion that say to not be a fool forever, to reject the laws of natural intellect and reasoning? I can imagine Hosea saying that most people would not have done this. But when he heard God speak, he obeyed. He had to. His love for God dictated it. Their fellowship warranted it. Their relationship justified it, and his purpose predicted it. He had to do what God said to do. He had to for the sake of Kingdom progression, as well as his continued relationship with Him. He knew whose he was.

When you hear God speak there are two things that you must do.

First, you must obey—no more and no less. You must simply do as He says in the exact way that He tells you to do it. You should journal your conversations with God because you will need to refer back to them often. If what God tells you to do involves other people, look and wait for the open door. God will even reveal to you where the door is located. Do not try to open it yourself, however, as you may do so prematurely.

Obeying God when you hear Him speak takes you into another realm with the Father. It opens the door for further fellowship and instructions. It deepens relationship. It shows that you trust God, and that you can be trusted.

It is important that we as children of God understand the importance of obeying God for the sake of our continued relationship with Him. When we receive an instruction, assignment, or mandate from God, we must remain in constant fellowship with Him so as to receive further instructions and directions concerning the assignment. With the assignment, we must be ushered into a realm to complete the task. How we respond to God in one realm will determine if we will go to the next, which is necessary to complete the current and future assignments given to us.

When you know God's purpose in you, when you hear God speak, you will not be motivated by the how or the why, but by God's will concerning you and the Kingdom. *Your consumption in God dictates your obedience to Him without compromise. You automatically yield to Him because of the very fact that you are in His presence. As a matter of fact, you are so glad and feel so privileged to be in His presence that whatever He says, you just obey.*

It is only after His presence is no longer upon you that you start getting goose bumps and say to yourself, *Now what did I just say yes to?*

Second, you must move into deeper depths of fellowship. This is imperative. Moving into deeper depths means higher levels of yielding. No matter how much you think you have been yielding to God, new instructions call for a new and deeper depth of yielding, in order to receive further instructions. So you must yield yourself specifically to that assignment and in all areas of your life concerning it.

Your deeper level of yielding means that your time spent with Him will be mostly spent in relation to your assignment. Your depth of revelation knowledge from God concerning your assignment, and even God Himself, will increase beyond your expectations. God will make you aware of His reasons and intents concerning some things relative to your assignment and the Church in general. It will actually be nothing new, just new to you. He will make known and clear His will and expectations of you, as well as your anointing, your mantle, and the repercussions you will face if you are disobedient. Your predestined territorial boundaries in the Spirit realm will be enlarged in your sight. And you will be released to operate within these preset boundaries. Grace and mercy will be at your beck and call. Principalities and rulers of darkness will know you by name. You will walk and operate in your kingly authority because God's purpose in you has been established and is being fulfilled.

While all of this is taking place, you will be fully aware that it's all about Kingdom building. It is all about God's will coming to fruition.

It's All About Love

> Jesus said, "For God so loved the world that He gave His only begotten Son, that whosoever believeth in him shall not perish but have everlasting life."
>
> John 3:16

The same motivating factor that God used to send Hosea to go and get Gomer is the exact same one that God Himself used to come through forty-two generations of the tribe of Judah and manifest Himself in the Person of His Son, Jesus Christ. And that factor was and still is love. It is God's love. It is His supernatural, burden-bearing, yoke-breaking, heart-mending, sacrificial love. It is the attribute that motivated God when He redeemed us.

For centuries, God has been trying to exemplify His love for mankind. He has been trying to help mankind to appreciate and understand the concept of godly, or *agape*, love. This love surpasses all human reasoning and understanding. This love is not based on our own capabilities, but rather on God's capabilities—who He is. Because God is love, the only thing that He can do is to express love. Despite our situation or condition, God's love speaks louder than sin, self-will, and self-depravation. It overshadows unfaithfulness and outweighs idolatry.

Love is who God is. All that He does and all that He is, is manifested through love.

Love is the epitome of God. It is His express image. Love is the only emotion and force that is available to us that can build, sustain, and maintain us. It is the moving force behind the creation and ongoing existence of mankind. When mankind had reached a point of no return and deserved only judgment and death, God's love manifested itself in the birth, life, death, burial, and resurrection of Jesus Christ. It cannot be measured, mastered, or mimicked by any other. It can only be expressed and experienced. It is our choice, our free will, even our decision, as to the extent we want this expression and experience manifested in our lives. "For God so loved the world that He gave His only begotten Son..." (John 3:16). In the offering of salvation to "whosoever will," the unsaved can experience God's love to the point of His crucifixion. The saved, those who have already come, can experience His love to the point of eternity.

Until they experience God's love as expressed through the cross, which is salvation, the unsaved will not experience it to the point of eternal and everlasting life. This is where the Church comes in. This is where we must go and get them and compel them to come to Christ. We must demonstrate God's expression of love, so that they, too, can experience the power of God's salvation, which is eternal and everlasting life.

The saved can experience the love and peace of walking in a relationship with God. And in this relationship, we can become intimate with Him, we can come to know Him and be kept by the sustaining power that only the love of One who loves unconditionally can provide.

This love is supernatural. It restructures, redefines, and defies the natural laws of reasoning, as well as the rules of compassion and commitment.

The only way that we can express or provide this type of love to any degree is to be conformed to the image of the Creator of a love of this type and magnitude, the Master and Creator of love itself, God.

This love is the love that God designed for the Church to demonstrate. This is the love that Jesus Christ spoke of in John 13:35, when He said, “By this all will know that you are My disciples, if you have love for one another.” Love is the “how” of the Great Commission: “Go therefore…” (Matthew 28:19). How? Love is the “how” in going to get Gomer. Love is the only source, the only tool that we need, because with it comes all else that is needed.

The Lord says, “Go again and get Gomer, the woman who cheated on Me. Never mind you, Hosea. But she cheated on Me. I loved her unconditionally, and she cheated on Me. I labored with her. I endured her unfaithfulness, her adulterous ways. I watched while she paraded other lovers before Me. I watched, even though she knew that I am a jealous God. She knew that I loathe adultery and idols. And now she’s down there with them as if I don’t exist. As if we never married nor entered into a covenant relationship. I have proved My love to her over and over again. Yet she still cheated on Me and left Me for another. But still, go again and get Gomer.”

There Is a Price to Pay for Gomer

> So I bought her for myself for fifteen shekels of silver, and one and one-half homers of barley.
> Hosea 3:2

We must understand that what God gives to the Church is for the specific reason of bringing souls to Christ, and dominating earth. Everything else that we obtain is a by-product of this priority.

The supernatural gifts, the ascension gifts, and the gifts of the Holy Spirit—as well as the natural gifts, talents, and manifestations of wealth and prosperity—are to be used for the specific purpose of bringing souls to Christ and glorifying God in doing it.

The manifestations of personal individual wealth and prosperity are a by-product of this Kingdom purpose. Fine houses, cars, clothes, and other possessions are good; after all we are kings, however, they must be demonstrated in good Godly taste and used properly. It is important that we do not confuse individual prosperity with Kingdom purpose, and place it first in focus and importance. For example, although some may disagree, there is nothing wrong with using wealth to purchase a plane to spread the Gospel of Jesus Christ. Just make sure that it is the true Good News that you are spreading, and not the "good news" of your own superiority. It would be robbery if it advertised you but forgot about God. Remember, you did not attain any of the wealth, but it was provided to you through His grace. This is to enable you to walk in the Kingdom authority and spread His Gospel, to win the lost and empower disciples.

So you must be careful to glorify God in all that you say and do, or in the process of time He will ground you and that plane.

In Hosea 3:2, he bought Gomer for himself for fifteen shekels of silver and one and one-half homers of barley. We must know that God has blessed the Body of Christ with what is needed to reclaim the lost and the broken.

What is needed to get the lost today?

First, God has given us gifts and ministry assignments.

We are engaged in a war. Christian ministry is the first demonstration of the Church's intent to engage in war against the enemy. It is a notice served to Satan concerning this engagement. The Church's presence here on earth lets the enemy know that we consider ourselves prepared for war. When we enter a rehab center or a prison, it puts demons on notice that we are here and that they must go. We bring the broken and lost to a point of wanting to be set free, and we free them by taking them by force from the enemy. Bishop T. D. Jakes said that they do not want to be like this, and I agree that they do not. But many do not know that they can be set free. Some cannot imagine the taste of freedom because they have been in bondage for so long and it has such a tight reign on their lives. Many need to see a soldier to even think of freedom. The Church must let them know that they can be free and that we are the soldiers who can set them free. Yes, they must be convinced that we can, indeed, free them. Many have not witnessed any truly great impact from the Church, so they do not have confidence in the power of the Church or their God.

We must use our spiritual weapons.

Second Corinthians 10:4 states that "the weapons of our warfare are not carnal but mighty in God for pulling down strongholds."

The armor is what we wear to protect us; the weapons are what we use to fight the enemy. What weapons in the supernatural have we been given access to for this warfare? Our armor guards us and allows us to stand against the wiles, tricks, and tactics of the devil. We can fight him off wearing the armor, but with what do we go on the offensive? We attack with our authority, faith, and the resources and power we have in the Kingdom of God.

We must use our God-given prosperity.

We often have the tendency to despiritualize prosperity preachers, when in reality, we must have prosperity—spiritual, physical, and financial—to fulfill God's purpose in our lives. God brings us provision by opening prosperity portals in the Spirit realm to be manifested in the natural so that we can buy what He commands us to buy and so that we can move about freely to dominate and further the Kingdom. With this prosperity, we can release wealth to others and bless others, as well as be blessed ourselves as a demonstration of God's ability and willingness to prosper His people. Our prosperity should be a testimony to the glory of God. It demonstrates how He provides for His Kingdom, as well as His people in it. We must not be so concerned with storing up wealth for ourselves or even our heirs; that we hold on to that which God has entrusted to us to sow into His kingdom to win and bless the lost and the broken, even to bless co-laborers in the Gospel. When God blesses you, you must be prepared to sow where He instructs you to sow.

What Hosea used to buy Gomer back with was the wealth that God had entrusted to him. Hosea understood that what was in his possession belonged to God. Likewise, what we hold in our possession belongs to God. Therefore, He decides what portion of what He has given us is to be sowed, to be released and what is to be retained for our own personal provision. We sow to reap. Whatsoever a man sows, so shall he also reap (see Galatians 6:7). We sow what has been given to us, what has been entrusted to us to transfer, on notice. We should not give much thought as to whether or not we will receive reciprocity for it, although we will, but we must understand that we are mainly holding it until the Holy Spirit instructs us where it is to go. We must not be consumed by the thought of receiving every time we give. God has already given us so much, including eternal and everlasting life.

Sowing should be motivated by and based on our assignment or purpose. We have because God has released, given, and imparted to us. He has strategically placed us at doors and in positions to prosper. This placement has been established in the Spirit realm. Doors that would not have been open otherwise, must open because their contents are supernaturally tied to, linked, or hooked up to His purpose in us and our assignment relating to it.

God had placed Hosea in the position to buy so that when the commandment came, Hosea could move without hesitation. Hosea still had what he needed. He had not spent it on material desires. He did not have to borrow it. This portion was God's. In the same way, our provision must be available when God speaks and commands us to do certain things with it.

Are you faithful in holding on to God's provisions, so that when He commands you to sow, it is there for His asking? Can God count on you to secure His treasure wisely until He calls for it?

Think about it. Would God bless you with millions and not expect you to sow a portion of it? Would He open up the windows of heaven and pour out upon you blessings that you do not have room enough to receive? That is overflow. We give out of the overflow both spiritually and materially. God gives us overflow so that we can sow to others who are already in and who are coming into the Body.

We sow out of faith and obedience. We sow from what we have and from what we have been entrusted with. We sow believing that we will receive. Whatsoever a man sows, that shall he also reap. We release because we are told by God to do so, whether we receive or not. It is more blessed to give than to receive. We must have an attitude of giving without focusing on receiving. When we release our wealth, we should not have the attitude of getting something in return, just for personal pleasure and prosperity, because pleasing God should be our reward. The act of obedience to God and knowing that we gave Him pleasure should be our reward.

We are not to be surprised when we must release what we have been holding for God for a specific purpose.

Church of God, God is speaking to us. He is saying, "Take what I have given you and do what I tell you to do with it." God is giving it to us, and when He comes for the release, He expects it to be there. Bank it, invest it, increase it, and just remember that soon you will be instructed to release it.

Not only must God's treasure be available for sowing and release, but this sowing dictates that it must be done where He commands it to be done. He has established it to be placed in fertile ground even if our natural eye does not see it. Hosea was commanded to use a portion to buy Gomer out of slavery at the marketplace. He had to purchase Gomer the prostitute, not Lucinda the accountant. God may tell you to release funds to a local shelter. This means that you cannot release the money to your cousin's dress shop. Your cousin needs to receive from your personal portion, not from God's holdings. In other words, do what you will with your portion, but God's portion must be directed toward the harvest. It must go where He sends it. It must be planted in the ground where God has established for it to grow.

I contend that most of the Church's prosperity is to be released into the harvest, while the remaining goes to the house of worship. It appears that quite the opposite is taking place. There seems to be a race to build the biggest and the finest sanctuaries or even TV ministries. This competition has left many communities untouched by the churches that are housed in them. This is why many communities are beginning to reject the presence of the Church, because instead of giving to the community, we are sucking from them, and they resent it. We suck their parking; we suck their tax base. Anyone in their position would be resentful. We build schools and daycares for our members who do not even live in the community, and we charge so much that not only can the community not afford to attend, many of our members can't, either. Our doors are locked tight and barred during the day when we could be running community programs with the ultimate goal of bringing souls to salvation and glorifying God while doing it.

Yes, we must charge to maintain our ministries and programs, but the burden is heavier for the Body, as well as the community, because the bulk of tithes are being spent on elaborate mortgages and musicians for entertainment.

Does your church have knowledge of or a listing of the group homes, rehab centers, shelters, and even prisons in your community? Do you have any idea as to the makeup of your community? How many homes have members who are imprisoned or in rehab centers or backsliders? How many in your congregation may be on the verge of backsliding because their problems have not been dealt with? Do you have a church representative who attends the community advisory neighborhood council meeting so that you are aware of the crime and other areas that the enemy may be controlling in the community? Have you discerned and assessed the demonic activity that operates in or controls your community? Have you gone to war for your community? Is your outreach limited to quarterly or monthly visits to the senior citizens' homes or share packages? Have you placed yourself in the position to hear God speak about His purpose for your church in relation to the community in which you are housed? Have you sought to network with other Christian churches to effect change in your community and bring souls to Christ? Have you taught, trained, and empowered your membership to minister and bring souls to Christ?

When the head walks in empowerment, then he can empower the Body and the Body can empower the broken and the lost.

It is not enough to go out on a street corner with our Bibles turned to Romans 10:9–10 and thrust pamphlets on the steps to salvation into the hands of passersby.

1. You must be in the right location.
2. You must have on the right armor.
3. You must possess the right weapons.

You must be careful whom you send. Do not send a private to fight a lieutenant's battle. There will be engagement in realms of demonic warfare around and even perhaps in an individual before they will even be able to consider Romans 10:9–10. If this is not dealt with first, their "salvation" will be a mere repetition of words, as opposed to them becoming saved for real.

Whenever you are dealing with the broken or the lost, there is always the presence of suppression, oppression, and often depression and possession. There will be a strongman that will have to be dealt with in the process of bringing a person to salvation or even into a stronger relationship with God. The enemy will have to be identified and defeated.

You have been predestined and ordained both corporately and individually to wage war on certain battlefields and in certain realms of the Spirit.

Hosea said, "So I bought her for myself for fifteen shekels of silver and one and one-half homers of barley" (2:3). It did not matter what Hosea wanted or did not want, but who was commanding him to do it. When he heard God's voice, he obeyed. In the manner in which God spoke, he bought Gomer back.

SPEAK INTO GOMER'S LIFE

> And I said to her, "You shall stay with me many days; you shall not play the harlot, nor shall you have a man—so, too, will I be toward you."
>
> Hosea 3:3

For us to be empowered, we must be walking and operating in Kingdom authority. Kingdom authority is the same realm of authority in which Jesus walked. The Father gave this authority to Jesus, and Jesus gave it to the Church, or the Body. The head cannot have authority, and the body not. It flows downward. This is the only way that we, the Church, can defeat the enemy. This is the only way that we can break yokes for the broken and the lost and empower them to do likewise. The power of God is in the Spirit realm because being in bondage is in the realm of the Spirit, and there is no other realm whereas we can do warfare and bring souls to Christ. This is why the weapons of our warfare are not carnal, because the war is in the Spirit realm, not the natural realm. The Church has been fighting in the natural. This is why we have not and are not having a greater impact on the earth. We seduce our youth with natural, worldly music, arguing that we must meet them where they are. They are in supernatural bondage, and we must meet them on the battlefield and take them from the enemy by force.

The boundaries and conditions of Kingdom authority in which each individual can operate has been established from their mother's womb. These dimensions and realms of authority are based on our level of assignment and the depth of the Spirit realm in which this assignment takes us. This depth dictates how far we will go in the heavenly realm. And how far we go in the heavenly realm dictates how far we will go into the realms of darkness to wage war on the enemy. We must be empowered by the Holy Spirit.

There are areas, boundaries, and dimensions of Kingdom authority that an individual will need to reach in order to fulfill God's purpose for their lives. Grace has been given the specifics and instructed to make them available to us.

Unless we have tapped into these dimensions and realms and are operating in them (dimensions are levels, or steps, and realms are depths per dimension that are only known and revealed by God), we will have little effect in ministry and in taking Gomer out of the clutched hands of the enemy.

Kingdom authority dictates, defines, and identifies our boundaries and the realms of demonic dominance we can overcome. When we say, "Lord, enlarge our territory," we are saying, "Lord, cause me to seek, and make known to me the boundaries in which I have been predestined to operate but have not reached the level of spiritual maturity and dominance I need to do so."

"Lord, enlarge my territory" means, "Lord, open my eyes so that I may see further in the Spirit realm, so that I may see what I do not see, but what has always been there. Lord, enlarge my view. Bring me into a place of fellowship, worship, and relationship with You so that I may see what has always been there. Take me to the top of my predestined mountain so that I can see all of my territory, my Promised Land. God, let me see all that You have purposed for me to do, to teach, to preach, to prophesy, to touch, to compel, to empower, to impart, to war against."

Not only was Hosea in a place to hear God, not only did he have and use what God gave him to take Gomer back, but Hosea had stepped into the dimension and realm of demonic dominance that was necessary to war for Gomer and complete his assignment and God's purpose for him. Even if Gomer's lover did not want to release her, he had to, because the dimension and realm that Hosea operated in dictated, effectuated, commanded, and demanded without compromise Gomer's release and freedom.

There was no demonic power, principality, or hierarchy operating in the realm necessary for Gomer's release that could war against Hosea's anointing and boundaries of authority in that realm and win.

And so it is with Kingdom people, you and I. As I said, our dimensions, realms, and boundaries in the Kingdom have already been established from our mothers' wombs. The when, where, how, and sometimes even why is revealed to us through revelation knowledge. This is done by the Holy Spirit at predetermined times and seasons of God, relative to Kingdom building and advancement. This revelation knowledge comes through a lifestyle of worship and fellowship—not just *casual* visits, but a *fervent* lifestyle.

This knowledge is the key to our empowerment. We must know the will, way, and instructions of God to move in Him. And we should not move unless we move in Him. This empowerment places us in the right position individually and corporately, and thus enables us through the Holy Spirit to combat the enemy and speak into Gomer's life. It enables us to speak into the lives of the broken and the lost. It is in this position that you realize and understand the power and principle of speaking life and death into a person's life or situation. You know now that life and death is, indeed, in the power of the tongue of the empowered believer and vessel of God. You know that now that you have helped Gomer empty her house, you must not leave it empty, but you must speak the fullness of the Holy Spirit in it. You must call forth the fruit of the Holy Spirit so that Gomer will not have her house invaded and taken over again. You now use the boldness and authority and take Gomer all the way. You speak with boldness, power, assurance, and clarity, piercing the dividing asunder of Gomer's soul and spirit, and you command her to live. Your shield of faith has now become a weapon of offense. You stretch it forth on attack, as well as on guard. You raise your sword, speaking into Gomer's spirit, into her life.

You continue to speak, as Hosea did. *Hosea spoke what Gomer would do next.* "And I said to her, 'You shall stay.'"

He spoke what she would do and established it. Hosea became Gomer's "midwife" and helped her birth the decision to choose life, to come to know the power of fellowhip. Fellowship, intimacy with God, is only productive when a person has decided within himself that he wants it. We must help others come to this decision by removing whatever blockage prevents them from making a conscious decision about their salvation.

Hosea allowed God to use him to birth a desire in Gomer, and then he helped her to identify the direction to her desire. He then established her future. Despite what comes before or against you, "you shall."

No matter what people say about you, "you shall."
No matter how hard things appear, "you shall."
No matter how you feel at any given time, "you shall."
No matter how much the enemy tries to tempt you, "you shall."

He established stability—"you shall stay." No more running here and there.
He spoke location—"you shall stay here with me." No more unfaithfulness and no more idol worship.

"You shall stay with me," the one who loves and sacrifices for you, despite your behavior.

Because Gomer had opened herself up for change, Hosea strategically took the time to set the path for her life and helped bring her into a renewed relationship with him, with the Father, with Jesus Christ, and with the Holy Spirit. You shall be stable, not remain marred.

"You shall stay with me many days." He established a time for her, as well. She would stay many days. He took authority and set the timing for Gomer by denouncing her instability and uncertainty. "Many days," he spoke, declared, and established.

By declaring "many days," Hosea set in order Gomer's steps. We must speak into the lives of the broken and the lost and usher them into a point of stability and certainty. We must empower and enable them to decide within themselves whom they will serve with the determination to spend eternal and everlasting life with Him.

When we speak, it must not be as sounding brass and tinkling cymbals. It must be certified, authenticated, and backed by the yoke-breaking power of the Holy Spirit. Absence of the manifested power of God would have made Gomer's experience a mere formality. She would have remained broken and lost, and Hosea would have had no effect on Gomer's life, bringing no glory to God and making no impact for the Kingdom.

Unfortunately, much of the Church's witnessing is more formality than empowerment. We cannot give what we do not have. Too many Christians are bound and suppressed themselves. Many are unhappy, unstable, uncertain, unfaithful, idol worshipers in denial and without peace.

I attended an evening service at a church a short while ago. At the end of the message, the preacher gave an altar call. Of several hundred people in the congregation, at least 95 percent went to the altar. As I watched the last ones approach the altar, I heard the Lord speak. He said, "So many have come to the altar because My people are not operating in Kingdom authority. One cannot bind, rebuke, and loose in someone else's life that which remains in theirs. Likewise, one cannot loose in someone else's life what is absent in his own." In other words, one must be delivered before he can deliver.

We, as leaders, must help people identify, stir up, and operate in the gifts and ministry assignments that God has placed inside of them and ordained for their lives.

When God asks the Church, "Who's going to get Gomer?" He is speaking to the leadership first.

Leaders, who are you sending, and how are you sending them? Are they coming back with Gomer, or are they returning empty-handed?

Leaders must train and equip their people. They must empower them to empower others. They must help them to understand that with empowerment comes joy and peace, access and resources. Leaders must help their sheep focus on God and not on themselves. While they may encourage them to respect leadership, they must discourage them from focusing on and honoring the leader himself, over God. Again, judgment begins at the house of God, to the head first. God will hold the leaders accountable for the growth and development of the sheep. We have been charged to lead the flock. And lead means just that—to lead. We must remember that sheep watch the shepherds and tend to go in the direction in which they are led.

Leadership does not just entail helping the laity maintain their own lives, but making sure that they receive the nourishment and empowerment to fulfill God's purpose in their lives.

Apostles, you will have to answer to God for those whom you send. You will be held accountable as to why you sent them and in what direction you sent them.

Pastors will have to answer for the nourishment of the sheep. Sheep must be fed the proper food so that they can endure and produce. Sheep follow the voice of the shepherd. They respond to the shepherd, whether it is for correction, instruction, or encouragement. Even if the shepherd is wrong, the sheep tend to follow him still.

All sheep are not to be on the same food regimen. When they are babies, they will eat baby food, so give them baby food. But you must be mindful that babies are born to grow. They must grow, so you must wean them off baby food and onto meat. Then when they learn how to walk, remember that they must walk somewhere, and for sheep, that somewhere is usually where their shepherds lead them.

Sheep must not just be told what to do; they must be compelled. To be compelled is inclusive of having information provided to them that aids them in making the right decision in any given situation.

When sheep are sent, do not send them to do an adult's job. You must first grow them to adulthood. The broken and the lost must be brought into fellowship with God. We must train, empower, and impart wisdom to the sheep so that they may go and get Gomer. They must speak into her life and bring her back home to the One who loves her.

In Hosea 3:3, the prophet said, "You shall not play the harlot." Hosea disallowed and denounced this activity from resurfacing in Gomer's life.

Despite being regarded as the spouse of Jehovah, Israel had chased after idols. They had become intimately involved in Balak worship. They built high places and worshiped other gods. Despite being the spouse of Jehovah, Israel had become the prostitute of Balak. They had flaunted their unfaithfulness before God, while observers wondered, "Why does He love her anyway? What does He see in her? After all that she has done to Him, how is it that He can still care?"

After his humiliation in going and getting Gomer, Hosea came against the spirit of perversion and idolatry and commanded Gomer not to volunteer herself to that perversion again.

And so it is with the Gomers of today, the broken and the lost. They have left their Creator and sought the affections of another. These Gomers will continue in this state unless and until the Church, the Body of Jesus Christ, goes and gets her and speaks into her life.

"Nor shall you have a man—so, too, will I be toward you" (Hosea 3:3).

The Lord says, "From henceforth, Gomer, your desire shall be for Me. When you go to bed at night and awaken each day, I will be the One whom you will desire. I will be the One whom you will see, and I will be the One whom you will want. Furthermore, I will think of you, as well. You, too, will always be on My mind. My thoughts will be toward you. I will desire to fellowship and be in relationship with you.

"You will not long for another, because you will have Me. You will remember the love that we have for each other. You will remember the covenant that we have one to another, and you will not break it. You will remember Me, and you will remember our covenant. You will remember My faithfulness to you, and you will be faithful to Me. We will be together forever."

The Tragedy of Gomer

> Now by chance a certain priest came down that road, and when he saw him, he passed by the other side.
>
> Luke 10:31

What Gomer was experiencing, as do most broken people today, is a lifestyle and condition that many Christians are spiritually unsympathetic about. This lack of concern and inability to relate can be primarily attributed to a lack of understanding about the tribulations of the broken, even though many of us have been or are currently in that very position ourselves.

The truth of the matter is that what the Gomers of today are going through can only be seen through the eyes of a truly compassionate heart. It can only be felt by one who, through either sympathy or empathy, understands the process, pain, passion, penalty, and penance of the broken.

Many would argue that Gomer deserved what she went through and that what the broken today are experiencing and will continue to experience as a result of their careless living is no one's fault but their own. To be where they are and finding themselves enslaved by a conniving, unloving, uncompassionate taskmaster named sin is a nightmare that they create and now must live through on their own.

Many people would argue that Gomer never should have left her husband, the one who loved, provided, and sacrificed for her. And she definitely should not have left her children. What real mother would? Many would argue that she should have known better.

As with Hosea, the Church's decision to help or aid the broken and the lost must not be made from our natural reasoning and understanding of the situation, but rather on what God is saying to do about it.

In Matthew 18:19, God said to go—He did not say to analyze and then go. He simply and clearly said to go. God's decision as to whom He will use as vessels to claim the lost and in what manner He will do so is His and His alone to make. God is sovereign, and He clearly makes that known to us in Jeremiah 1:5.

Jeremiah clearly records that we have been formed by the thought process of God. Our purpose, destiny, and anointing is predetermined by Him, as well. While we were still in our mothers' wombs, according to His foreknowledge of us, God created a future for us out of our past. This is a future that is devoid of natural reasoning or compromise. What God has formed cannot be unformed, changed, or altered.

A tragedy of Gomer's, it would seem, is what she is going through even today. The effects of the errors, mistakes, bad choices, and decisions that she made. However, I contend that the real tragedy of the Gomers in the world is not how they got in the condition or position that they are in, but rather that no one has gone to get them out. You see, there is no doubt that what Gomer is going through can change for the better, but this will happen only when she is taken out of the grasp of the enemy by the saints of God. Believers must take her back, by utilizing all of the natural and spiritual resources that God has given them access to.

We must not be concerned as to where they are or how they got there, but only the fact that they are lost and broken, that they have been for too long, and that we must go and get them. Yes, the tragedy of Gomer is that the Body of Christ, it seems, has turned a deaf ear to God's command to "go therefore" and get Gomer. Yes, we have turned a deaf ear to people who are crying out for help. This deafness is a result of our not walking in the power and authority that God has ordained and called us to walk in. We must be aware that if we have not heard God, then we have not heard the lost. We must provide help to the broken and the lost, and this help can only be obtained and released through an anointed, empowered child of God. This is help that today's average Christian is not able or equipped to provide.

The government or even philanthropists in our society can give food, shelter, clothing, and even counseling, but only an empowered child of God can bind and loose, rebuke and cast out demons principalities and powers of darkness. We are the only ones who can identify and destroy the strongholds that are proclaiming that Gomer belongs to them and that they will not release her under any circumstances.

Body of Christ, we do not need the enemy to let them go; we have the power to take them by force. Yes, we do. We have been given access to the tools we need, which are love and the yoke-breaking power of God, given to us in order to rescue Gomer. The tragedy, as I said, is that we are not accessing and exercising this love and power to reclaim Gomer and for the Kingdom.

The most profound tragedy of Gomer is that she was out of fellowship with God. She had become a breaker of the covenant. Her isolation was symbolic of the exile of Israel from God. Gomer, as with those who are broken and out of fellowship with God today, depict the tragedy of someone turning his back on his Creator, on the One who loves and sacrificed for him.

This tragedy of isolation caused Israel to become separated and out of fellowship with the very One who gave birth to them. And the absence of fellowship with their Creator provoked God to declare that there are certain rights and privileges that they must be denied.

The first is the privilege of access to the kingly anointing and the rights that are readily available to those who are in relationship with God.

The Lord says, "You shall be without king or prince. Although you have proven over and over again that you need it, you shall not have anyone to rule over you, to provide for you, or to protect you from the snares and attacks of the enemy. During your isolation, you will not have it easy. You must be denied certain things because of your covenant violations. For Me to be your King while you are in violation of My Word would then make Me a violator of My Word, as well.

"Not only will you be without king or prince, but you will not be allowed to wear My priestly garments, which bore your ancestral affiliation and ties inscribed in them. This denial symbolizes My disownment of you. To reverse My decision, you will have to prove yourself to Me. In doing so, you will experience being cut off from your places, things, and gods of worship. You must, through all of this, be to Me and I will be to you for many days. Afterward, you can and will return to Me. You will have to come to a point where you will deny the very things for which you left Me. This is true repentance. It is a complete turning away from the things for which you left Me. You must do to them what you did to Me. Amid temptation, you must deny the idols that you had submitted yourself to and give honor and admiration instead to Me. You must not build altars to them or carve their images. You must not be their prostitute or slave. But for many days, during your isolation, you must be to Me."

When a person becomes bound by a relationship, situation, or condition, it is not something that they can just walk out of when they decide to. The bondage has its origin in sin, and a person must realize that sin is a hard-hitting and hard-fighting taskmaster that has no intention of setting them free. Within sin, there lies demonic presence and influences that have been perpetuated by demon forces and principalities in conjunction with the world system to keep an individual in bondage.

When people are out of the covering relationship with their King, then they are "open range" for the enemy. Until they are reunited with their King, they are under control of the enemy. And they will be so for many days. This is why it is pivotal that the Body of Christ reclaim Kingdom territory by gathering the lost whom the enemy has taken into captivity.

While they are lost, they are without the provision, protection, leadership, and rulership that a King provides. We are all under supernatural rulership. And if we are not under God's authority, then we are under the devil's.

God allowed Israel to be taken into captivity. During their captivity, He placed on them certain criterion for returning to Him. While under the pressure of being in a foreign country and being exposed to and tempted by the same idol worship and lifestyle they clung to, they had to resist becoming partakers again. In other words, they had to be true in their acts of repentance. This meant turning their backs on the very things that got them into trouble with God in the first place.

Many broken people, the unsaved, the carnal, and the backslidden, are out of relationship with God. In order for them to come into the kingly anointing that God wants for them, there has to be a turning away from the sins that have led them into various areas and conditions of bondage. There has to be a renunciation of the idols and the unholy lifestyle that they have clung to and become bound to.

The broken and the lost today, as with Israel, and yes, even as were all of us, have entered into a supernatural aspect of warfare that is far beyond their comprehension and control. They, too, must be brought out by a supernatural power that exceeds the realm of what has them in bondage. This power must exceed those to whom they have pledged their allegiance. And the only power greater than anyone or anything, both natural or supernatural, is the power of God. God's power is the only yoke-breaking power available to mankind.

Body of Christ, the only way that the lost are going to return to God, and come into an intimate, empowered relationship with Him, is if we, as Hosea did with Gomer, go and get them.

Afterward the Children Shall Return

> Afterward the children of Israel shall return and seek the Lord their God and David their King.
> Hosea 3:5

Afterward you shall return. After you have put your worship habits in the right perspective. After you have ceased building altars and carving idols. After you have denied those things that you have clung to and allowed to separate you from God. After you have spent many days in isolation and separated from your Creator. After you have considered the love that you thought you had and the love that you lost. After you hunger and thirst after righteousness. After you realize that you cannot sing the songs of the Lord in a strange land.

After you have come to yourself and realize that you shall worship the Lord your God and Him only shall you serve. Then you shall return.

The enemy uses every weapon and opportunity that he can to prevent a worship relationship from developing between God and His love, mankind.

What also hinders an individual from living life eternal here on earth and walking in God's divine authority and destiny is a worship relationship with God. So, if the enemy can keep an individual in bondage to him, then that person will not be worshiping God. But if we, the Body of Christ, will raise our worship to higher dimensions and deeper realms, God will empower us, and we will be able to war with the enemy in our own lives and on the behalf of others. We will take authority and walk in it with boldness and fervor. We will understand that our armor is not made just to withstand the wiles of the devil, but to go on the offensive into his camp and the territories that he has illegally taken hold of.

When a person's worship is toward God, then and only then will he seek Him, seek the fulfillment of His covenant, and fear Him and His goodness.

Worship ushers people into the presence of God. Once you experience His presence, you will seek Him. You are drawn by more revelation of Him every time you experience His presence—so much so that you will seek Him every chance you get. And when it seems as though you cannot get a chance, you will make a chance. You will miss *New York Undercover* and *American Idol*. Your reality show will no longer be *Big Brother* but *Abba Father*. You will not hang out with your friends as much. Your desires will change, and time management will almost become an obsession with you. Rather than worship being fit in around the comings and going of your day, the comings and goings of your day will be centered around your lifestyle of worship and your ability to spend quality time seeking the glory, the Person, and the attributes of God. *The more you seek Him, the more of Him you will seek.* Soon you will no longer be motivated by signs and wonders or miracles and gifting, but rather the glory, the Person, and the presence of God. You will find that you can neither start nor end your day without having been in fellowship and worship with Him.

Not only will you seek Him, but you will become zealous about seeing His covenant promises fulfilled. "Your throne will never be without a king," states the Davidic covenant promise. You will want to come into your kingly anointing, which include the rights and privileges associated with ownership and rulership. As a result of the meritorious acts of Jesus Christ, the last and forever King to grace King David's throne, we, the Body of Christ, have been given ownership and rulership over the Kingdom of earth, whereas we access our authority in heavenly places. We have authority to bind and loose in Jesus Christ's name.

Not only will we seek God in His glory and strive for the fulfillment of the Davidic promise, but we will also fear Him. We will have a reverential awe for Him that can only be understood by an empowered child of God. This awe epitomizes respect, honor, faithfulness, holiness, fellowship, relationship, worship, and reverence. This awe comes to us because of Him. We receive it because of who He is: sovereign Creator; the beginning and the end; Alpha and Omega; from everlasting to everlasting; omniscient, omnipresent, omnipotent God. This awe is accompanied by a fear of not pleasing Him. You long to please Him, so you fear displeasing Him. You long for His presence, so you fear being out of it. You fear being separated and isolated from the One whom you love and for whom you long. You understand that once you are made privy to revelation knowledge, then there are certain things that He will not tolerate from you.

You fear His goodness. It follows you all the days of your life. You are aware that when you are out of the will of God, goodness will expose you, your sinfulness, your flaws, and your frailties.

But the lost and the broken shall return to God, their Creator. After many days of suffering, agony, pain, and enslavement, they shall have the yoke-breaking power of God released in their lives by the saints of God. Then they shall return to Him.

He That Hath an Ear, Let Him Hear

"Hear the word of the Lord",...

Hosea 4:1a

God has given you an ear to hear. So, hear you must!

Hear the word of the Lord, Body of Christ, for the Lord has brought a formal charge against you. Thus saith the Lord, "Tell My people that they are not walking in Kingdom authority, and because of this, the lost are still lost and the broken are still broken. I am commanding My people to come into fellowship and relationship with Me. They must worship Me so that I can loose the power inside of them that has been granted to them from their mother's womb."

Hear the word of the Lord, for God is speaking to His Body. Your hearing has become dulled because of your unholy and unharmonious lifestyles, as well as your lack of worship.

You have allowed your ears to become itchy for the sounds of the world and have not heard God. But I speak to you this day. The Lord is moving through the Body of Christ like a mighty rushing wind. As a chariot of fire, He is moving throughout the sanctuaries of His people. He is stretching forth

His arm throughout the Body. And he that hath an ear will hear. God is going to sharpen your dulled hearing, because after He speaks, He will speak no more.

Oh, what a joy when the Church fully realizes the plans that God has for man, when they realize and understand the true concept of purpose, principles, and power.

Purpose is God's predestined plans for His people, in relation to building, restoring, and maintaining His Kingdom here on earth.

Principles are the rules and guidelines under which we must operate to fulfill this purpose.

Power is the motivating, operating force that allows and enables us to move in the supernatural realm and complete God's assignment here on earth.

Israel failed God. Their unfaithfulness and lack of devotion prohibited them from tapping into the resource that they needed to complete God's purpose in them. This resource was the revelation knowledge of God.

God had made a promise to Moses saying, "...they shall be My people, and I will be their God." (see Jeremiah 24:7) The words *my* and *your* are words that suggest ownership or possession. And out of this is birthed fellowship, relationship, love, devotion, faithfulness, nurture, gentleness, kindness, understanding, respect, and honor. These are qualities and attributes that must be practiced and demonstrated by both parties of the covenant. God was and still is infallible in His practice and demonstration of all of these qualities. But Israel left much to be desired.

Israel had failed God horribly and as a result had to be corrected. This is true of many people in the Church today. Without correction, the Kingdom will suffer. Where did Israel go wrong? Where is the Church going wrong today?

1. They became breakers of the covenant.
2. They did not desire mercy or truth.
3. They did not know God.
4. They broke restraint.

Through His prophet Hosea, as well as through other prophets of that era, God made it clear that there are certain fallacies that have hindered and eventually stopped the Church from being productive in Him. These fallacies have caused the program of God to become misrepresented.

God has provided a place of worship in which we may hear His voice. It is when our hearing becomes dull that He must use His prophets to make His voice heard by a stubborn, dulled ear.

In Hosea 4:1, God used Hosea to give a command to a particular group. The command was to hear, and the group was the people of Israel. Israel heard through this prophet that because of their unfaithfulness, they had neglected to fellowship with God. Fellowship breeds worship, relationship, and communication.

The Lord, in essence, said to Israel: "I am bringing a charge against you. You have become a covenant-breaker. I have been your God, but you have not been My people. Instead, you have played the harlot. You have pledged yourself to Me, but your heart has been far from Me. You have not kept your marriage vow; instead, you have left Me for another. I am bringing this charge against you because you must be made aware of your sins. You must be chastised for your sins and corrected so that you will sin no more."

The court in which Israel was to be judged was the high court of the universe, and this would not be a trial by a jury of their peers. They would be tried by the high authority of the court, God.

There is a three-count indictment.

First, they did not desire truth. In Romans 1:18, the apostle Paul clearly revealed that mankind holds down, or suppresses, the truth about God in unrighteousness. He wrote that the truth that has been taught or revealed to us is held down, or hidden, from the sight of those who have not come into the knowledge of the truth about God. In other words, the love that we have seen God demonstrate cannot be seen by others because we, the Body, being the vessels of demonstration by God to those outside of the Body, have taken the love and placed it on the backburners of our hearts. We have instead shown rudeness, pride, arrogance, irritability, impatience, unkindness, and the like. We have blocked the world's view of God. We have ignored the fact that what the broken and the lost can neither see nor experience, they cannot know.

In addition, unholy lifestyles and the mistreatment of God, or unrighteousness and ungodliness before others, has created a revolving-door lifestyle for people already in and those coming into the Church. God has been robbed of fellowship with His creation, and the broken and unsaved have been deprived of knowing the power of the resurrection of Jesus Christ. They are deprived of seeing the yoke-breaking essence of God demonstrated to them, and God has brought an indictment against the Body of Christ for allowing this to happen.

Bishop Paul Morton, Bishop of Full Gospel Baptist Church Fellowship, says that the Kingdom is under attack, and he asks the question, "What are we going to do about it?"

God says that we must be brought into correction so that we may walk in Kingdom authority. We cannot ward off the attack against the Kingdom unless we can operate in the realm of Kingdom authority where the attacks are taking place. The Church is fighting in the flesh, while the enemy is running rampant in the realms where deliverance of the lost must take place. The Church is not operating in the realm where spiritual authority is needed to get Gomer—the lost, the broken—out of the clutches of the devil. They are not operating in Kingdom authority.

Instead, they are in the realm of strife, confusion, wounding in the local church, adultery, fornication, lack of prosperity, pride, and a music industry running out of control, while Gomer is crying, "Who's going to come and get me?"

Second, Israel had no mercy or devotion. We have come to the point, like Israel, where God cannot count on us to do anything. If it does not benefit us, then we do not want to have anything to do with it. Devotion and faithfulness is a by-product of love. If a person has a problem being faithful or devoted to someone with whom they are in a covenant or marriage relationship, then more often than not, their love is lacking.

When we lack devotion, it is directly related to the depth of love for the one with whom we have entered into covenant relationship. In Israel's case, as with the Church today, the lack of love for God has a lot to do with it.

When you are truly devoted to someone, you do not let anyone or anything interfere with your relationship with that person. But if you wander, then you are said to be out of covenant.

Israel wandered both spiritually and physically. They physically built and set up high places, and they spiritually entered into worship relationship with pagan or idol gods. What an indictment. Israel, as with Gomer, had become indifferent to God's feelings.

What about us? What about the Church today? Have we not become indifferent and insensitive to God's feelings? Have we not become unresponsive to His demands and commands? Do we not build and set up high places, too—places that we elevate before God in our minds and worship with our hearts? Do we not set ourselves above God and yield to our every fleshly whim? Do we not place our children and pastors on pedestals and are crushed when they disappoint us? That's your god, if you do. Where is the Church's music? Have we not placed the world's music above the melodies that God has birthed in our hearts? We have said that the world's music is better and more effective for our youth, when in reality, there is no yoke-breaking power behind it. All we have done is taught the youth how to worship music and give honor and homage to the idols behind it. Do not fool yourself; there are idol spirits attached to much of the music that we are bringing before our congregations and the ears of God.

Third, Israel had no knowledge of God. When someone does not recognize authority, they are sure to err in their relationship with the one who has authority over them. They will disrespect, dishonor, and surely wander from them sooner or later. They will not depend on them and will not honor the covenant that is between them. They will not recognize God as the authoritative leader and power in their lives.

Israel was guilty of the charges brought against them by the God of the universe. And I submit to you that the Church today is, too.

It is a tragic situation when the God of the universe, your Creator, the One who loves you and is devoted to you more than anyone else, brings charges against you. When you reach this point, then you have surely pushed God to the point of having to correct you. This is a tragic point for you. You cannot be effective in a covenant relationship with someone when you do not recognize their position in your relationship. How can you have confidence in the fulfillment of the covenant, if you do not have confidence in the partner in the covenant? Where is the trust?

Israel rejected the confidence that was available to them in God, so God withdrew any confidence that He had imparted to Israel. This confidence would have allowed them to fulfill their promise or part of the covenant.

Body of Christ, we do not want God to remove the grace that He has given us to fulfill our covenant relationship with Him. We are prone to wander, but to completely wander away is another story. Failure to recognize the authority in our lives is indicated by the breaking of any of the commandments. The commandments that God has given us to live by and has expressed and made clear are necessary to please Him and to enter into eternal rest and reward in Him. In Hosea 4:2, the prophet spoke forth words from God—that Israel's neglect to recognize God's authority as the initiator and head in the covenant was indicative of the breaking of some of the commandments. They were swearing and using God's name incorrectly and inappropriately. Other commandments violated included lying, killing, stealing, and adultery.

Body of Christ, we will pay for our unfaithfulness to God. We do not want God's wrath to manifest upon the Church. We do not want to have to suffer to obey. Unfortunately, however, suffering seems to be a position that man has to be in before he can hear God. God has given His Body an ear to hear, and they must hear.

With Gomer, as with Israel, they had to suffer hardship. But this is the love and faithfulness of God being demonstrated. Instead of wiping you out, letting you die, or allowing you to remain in a state of opposition to God, a state of being unproductive, God's love and devotion for you is exemplified in His careful and intentional plans. He allows you to wallow in your own choices and decisions, and then He brings you out and back to Him. For God to intervene at any point other than this would be a violation of your free will and your covenant relationship. So God must allow you to suffer much of life's consequences, choices, and decisions. However, He remains faithful and just to forgive and restore.

The breaking of certain commandments caused Israel to cross the boundary of the measure of grace that God had set, or predestined, for them in this situation.

The repercussions, or the effects, of your unfaithfulness include the following:

1. The land will mourn—and you will mourn. You will moan, groan, and cry out like a woman in travail. You will put on sackcloth and ask yourself, *How did it all come to this?* You will blame others, and they will blame you, without ever coming to a concrete answer or agreement. The ground will long to be fertile and produce. You will go to eat from it, and nothing will be there. You will call out, and no one will answer. Everyone will be sorrowful. They all will be in mourning, too.
2. There will be a wasting away of every living thing. Even the birds and fowl of the air, the beasts of the land, and the fish of the sea will suffer because of your unfaithfulness. All will suffer. All will waste away and be left without honor or prestige. You will look up and see that your so-called friends will be gone and that your idols were never there at all. You will be left with nothing but a covenant relationship to which you were unfaithful. You will be left with a covenant agreement without relationship. There will be a lack of provision, and you will be devoid of productivity. You will only think negative thoughts about yourself and those whom you felt played a part in getting you where you are.

> There will be a sorrowful, even pitiful, lack of provision. All that you thought would produce for you will become barren. You will cry and long to be where you were before—in covenant relationship with your God and Creator; in a covenant relationship where you were stable and secure; in a covenant relationship where you were confident and felt loved and cherished; where there was shelter and nourishment and health; where there was comfort and peace.

The Church will undergo a period of suffering if it does not hear the word of the Lord. We long for the end times to come, but what about the now times? We must handle the now before we can embrace the end.

They Will Sin No More

> "My people ask counsel from their wooden idols, and their staff informs them. For the spirit of harlotry has caused them to stray, and they have played the harlot against their God."
>
> Hosea 4:12

Body of Christ, if we go and get Gomer, the broken and the lost, and do to her as God did to Israel, through Hosea, we will have fulfilled God's purpose for us, both individually and corporately.

They will sin no more; instead they will worship God. As a deer pants by the water brooks, the broken and the lost will pant after God. They will know that God is love and that He loves them. They will long for His comfort and fellowship. They will experience intimacy and relationship. They will know God and the power of His resurrection. They will worship Him and no other.

The spirit of idolatry, which has caused them to stray, will cause them to stray no more. Yes, adultery, idol worship, sexual promiscuity and perversion, murder, lying, cheating, stealing, abuse, and molestation will no longer be the course of the day.

When the Church fulfills God's purpose here on earth, Jesus Christ will return, and man will sin against God no more.

Because of this, Gomer's heart will no longer be enslaved to sin, and there will come a time when the Gomers of the world will sin no more. This will be because the people of God heard and obeyed the Lord. They went and got Gomer. They compelled her to come into the fold, the family, the Body of Christ.

They realized that God has a purpose and a plan for mankind that extends far beyond the natural boundaries of earth, but it extends upward into the Kingdom realm, where God Himself dwells.

Not only will the Gomers of now sin no more, but all believers will be free from the presence of sin. All who believe in the Gospel of Jesus Christ will be ushered into the realm of freedom from sin. The presence and power of sin will be no more, and we all will come into the knowledge of the Kingdom of God and live an eternal and everlasting life.

We will boldly profess, "I have kept the faith, I have finished my course, and henceforth there is laid up for me a crown of righteousness." (see 2 Timothy 4:7) We will hear our Creator say, "Well done, My good and faithful servant, well done. You have been faithful over a few things, and now I will make you rulers over much." (see Matthew 25:21)

We will hear the angels' melodies as they sing hallelujah. We will step before the eternal presence of God and cry, "Abba, Father, we are here. We are here before You, before Your great and powerful throne. We examined our state and the state of Gomer. We panted after You in fellowship and worship and developed an intimate relationship with You. We understood the concept of divine purpose, and when we heard You speak, we obeyed. We paid the price to disciple Gomer, and we spoke into Gomer's life. We assessed the tragedy of Gomer and sought for her return. We used our ears to hear You, Father, and now many who were broken and lost will sin no more."

PRAYER OF RENEWAL

Oh my God and my Father, My Lord and my Saviour, how I long to know you and to please you. You are holy and awesome. You are my creator.

Make me to know you so that I may please you. Make me to know you so that I will walk in kingdom authority and fulfill your purpose in me.

Lord God Almighty, I realize and understand that I have not been doing all that I should in relation to my responsibility to you and to the broken and the lost.

I am aware that Matthew 28:18,19 records your command for me to go, yet I have not gone.

I have not consistently gone before you in worship and prayer. I have not been in fellowship with you enough to establish a genuine relationship that is necessary to learn of and fulfill your purpose in me.

I am sorry Father. Bring me now, I pray thee, into the right relationship with you and cause me to know your purpose in me and anoint and empower me to fulfill it.

I love you God and I want to dominate earth and the world as you have ordained the Body of Christ to do. Take me into the depths of your dimensions and realms, of revelation knowledge, so that I may know you more.

I submit every part of myself to you for your created purpose.

Thank you Father, in Jesus' name I pray, Amen.

To order additional copies of

WHO'S GOING TO GET GOMER?

have your credit card ready and call
1 800-917-BOOK (2665)

or e-mail
orders@selahbooks.com

or order online at
www.selahbooks.com

Contact Prophetess Janice Fountaine

Kingdom Empowerment Church/
Birthed For Purpose Ministries
6103 Baltimore Avenue, T-4
Riverdale, Md. 20747
(301) 277-1946 voice
(301) 277-1947 fax
Fountainej@aol.com
www.jfountaineministries.com
www.kingdomenpowermentchurch.com
www.bfpministries.com

www.ingramcontent.com/pod-product-compliance
Lightning Source LLC
LaVergne TN
LVHW020649100826
845148LV00012B/2392

* 9 7 8 1 5 8 9 3 0 1 8 6 3 *